Other Titles by Patricia Smith

To Weep For a Stranger: Compassion Fatigue in Caregiving

Healthy Caregiving: A Guide to Recognizing and Managing Compassion Fatigue – Presenter Guide Level I

Healthy Caregiving: A Guide to Recognizing and Managing Compassion Fatigue – Student Workbook Level I

Available from Healthy Caregiving, LLC
www.healthycaregiving.com

Compassion Satisfaction:

50 Steps to Healthy Caregiving

Compassion Satisfaction:

50 Steps to Healthy Caregiving

by Patricia Smith

A publication of the
Compassion Fatigue Awareness Project
www.compassionfatigue.org

DEDICATION

To my three children-
Blake, Derek and Elizabeth

"To the world you may be one person; but to one
person you may be the world."
– Dr. Seuss

ACKNOWLEDGMENTS

I am fortunate to have faithful family and friends who have walked this path with me from the beginning more than 12 years ago. First and foremost, to my family, especially my mom, Gloria, and my sisters, Ann and Terry, who are my caregivers and best friends. My friends Beth Nikels, Ann Straw, Joan O'Rourke, and Carin Jacobs who continue to offer a listening ear. And to my special friends Rick Swan, who is always present to me all the way from Lake Tahoe; Dr. Beth Hudnall Stamm, a consummate and generous professional who has given her life's work to help caregivers navigate the healing process; and Dennis Portnoy, San Francisco therapist and compassion fatigue expert who patiently answers all my questions whenever I call. Lastly, cover photograph is courtesy of Joy Imboden Overstreet.

I send my thanks and love to all of you.

CONTENTS

SECTION TWO: FOR THOSE IN YOUR CARE

SECTION THREE: FOR YOUR ORGANIZATION

INTRODUCTION

In 2000, an Oregon hospital inaugurated an in-house program called *No One Dies Alone*. The purpose of the program was to provide companionship and care to a dying person when no family members or friends existed or couldn't be present. Often, the need for this service is requested by a member of the chaplain services staff who is called in to comfort the person or, in Catholic hospitals, provide Last Rites. Compassionate Companions, as these program volunteers are called, receive training and schedule caregiving rituals where they are present onsite with the person anywhere between 1 - 36 hours. The program caught on and is now offered throughout hospitals and hospices nationwide.

In my health care public relations work, I interviewed a number of associates who volunteer for the *No One Dies Alone* program in one of the hospitals where I serve. What I learned was surprising to me. I believe it will be surprising to you, too.

I now understand caregiving practices are not static, they are constantly changing. The old tradition of one human taking full responsibility of providing care to another human is slowly fading away. In its place is a new concept embracing the idea of partnership, where both the caregiver and the person receiving care work together to affect hope and healing. And more important, if the person is able, both persons work together to make informed decisions such as treatment options and end-of-life preferences. (*I use the term "person" for expediency's sake to cover anyone who is receiving care depending on the helping profession. This could include a client, ward or family member, a friend, companion or partner. In some cases, it might even include a dog, cat or bird, if the caregiver is an animal welfare worker and ideas presented in the book are possible.)*

Since publication of my first book, *To Weep for a Stranger: Compassion Fatigue in Caregiving* in 2009, I have learned much more about both caregivers and the art of healthy caregiving. Between presenting workshops to helpers in myriad professions and answering emails from caregivers worldwide, I have come to realize the width and breadth of this very human interaction we call caregiving.

This new model of providing healthy care to others is emerging across the helping professions as well as with family caregivers. No longer is caregiving seen as a one way street – that is, one human being serving another human being who is incapacitated, in pain, suffering or preparing to die. True compassionate, healthy care is now viewed as a two-way street – that is, while being of service to another, a caregiver is called upon to be the receiver and bearer of the "gifts" the suffering impart to those who cross his or her path including medical professionals, family members, friends or religious. Those needing care are also encouraged to retain their personal power and take charge of their own health and well-being, to whatever extent possible.

In the new mode of caring, which is person-centered, persons hold up their end of the process and take an active role in allowing their lives, no matter how debilitating, to retain a level of quality and dignity. They are asked not only to appreciate and value the care they are receiving, but they are also being asked to reciprocate in kindness, patience and respect. A quality of life remains no matter how dire the circumstances. For a caregiver, there is much to be learned from those in pain and suffering and those about to die. And for those in pain, who are suffering and perhaps in the process of dying, there is a wealth of wisdom to be shared.

I have worked many years for a health system that promotes holistic wellness: body, mind and spirit. Physicians, nurses and associates who work for this health system respect all persons, particularly those who live in poverty. The everyday work ethic is based on the idea that a person actually enters into a healthy caring relationship with his or her care providers. The relationship is based on respect, trust and honesty – a partnership where everyone involved does his or her best to create both a culture of curing as well as a culture of caring that works both ways.

I don't believe there is a helper or caregiving organization or business that wouldn't want to embrace this ideal. Mutual respect, trust and honesty lead to better communication, effective listening, fewer incidents of abuse, less stress and burnout, and most important for the purposes of this book, lower levels of compassion fatigue and higher levels of compassion satisfaction.

Dr. Beth Hudnall Stamm, director, Institute of Rural Health at Idaho State University, has spent her professional career creating the Professional Quality of Life Self-Test (www. proqol.org). This test is the best tool available to measure compassion fatigue, burnout, secondary trauma, and compassion satisfaction in the caregiver. Dr. Beth encourages caregivers to download her test, free of charge. It is my suggestion caregivers take the test frequently.

Latest studies show that the most effective way to lower compassion fatigue scores, along with practicing authentic, sustainable self-care, is to raise compassion satisfaction scores. What exactly is compassion satisfaction? According to Dr. Hudnall Stamm: "Compassion Satisfaction is the pleasure we derive from being able to do our work well. Higher levels of Compassion Satisfaction are related to our ability to be effective caregivers."

I was moved to write *Compassion Satisfaction: 50 Steps to Healthy Caregiving* with these two new concepts in mind: Person and caregiver working in tandem to create healthy caregiving, and the possibility of a helper raising his compassion satisfaction level by being more effective in his caregiving practices and outcomes.

The *50 Steps to Healthy Caregiving* portion of this book presents 50 strategies followed by helpful suggestions to aid helpers and organizations in creating authentic, sustainable caregiving practices. All of the *50 Steps* begin with an action word. *Inspire. Create. Design. Learn. Develop.* In order to be change agents, we must take the first step and act. There will be work involved in meeting your caregiving tasks half way – or all the way, in some cases. But the outcome will surprise you, motivate your person, promote partnerships, and bring a new level of success to the work you have chosen to do. And most important, raise your compassion satisfaction scores!

The time has passed for fretting, worrying, thinking and damning the way things are. The time has come to do something about it. In the words of Albert Einstein, it's time to raise our voices and make a difference.

To those in need of care, thank you for respecting your helpers and realizing they are serving you from a place of empathy and compassion. To caregivers everywhere, thank you for the tenacity and passion with which you care for others! And thank you for the good work you do. I hope the ideas in *Compassion Satisfaction: 50 Steps to Healthy Caregiving* become a valuable resource for you now and in the future.

Patricia Smith
Founder & Director
Compassion Fatigue Awareness Project
Friday Harbor, San Juan Islands, WA
May 5, 2012

HOW TO USE THIS BOOK

Compassion Satisfaction: 50 Steps to Healthy Caregiving is written as a reference book. Take the advice of any one suggestion and you will have improved the quality of your caregiving tenfold. The more ideas you put into practice from these pages, the more satisfying your work will become. Due to the research of Dr. Beth Hudnall Stamm, director, Institute of Rural Health, Idaho State University, we now know high levels of compassion satisfaction counteracts the debilitating set of symptoms called Compassion Fatigue. According to Dr. Hudnall Stamm, compassion satisfaction is the pleasure we derive from being caregivers. This book was written as an aid in helping you raise your compassion satisfaction levels.

This book is divided into three specific sections. The first section is FOR YOU, THE CAREGIVER. These pages are dedicated to those who provide care with two thoughts in mind: hopefully, the ideas will generate new, energizing ways to offer care, but also suggests important steps for caregivers to practice authentic, sustainable self-care.

Section Two is FOR THOSE IN YOUR CARE and their family and friends. I know for many of you, your "person" is your mother, father, partner, or client. I use the term "person" throughout the book for want of a better term. Hopefully, the 15 suggestions help you engage your person and his or her loved ones in taking an active role in the caregiving processes.

The ideas were created to keep the big picture in focus and encourage those in our care to continue to embrace life.

Finally, Section Three is FOR YOUR ORGANIZATION. Put these 14 steps into action and you will build a more cohesive team working together to provide quality care while keeping staff members healthy and committed to their work.

In the back of the book you will find a section entitled: My Steps to Healthy Caregiving. This is the place where you can document ideas and thoughts concerning caregiving steps that have worked well in your specific environment. You may be surprised by your successes. If so, please connect with the Compassion Fatigue Awareness Project (CFAP). There is nothing we enjoy more than hearing your caregiving stories.

You can post your ideas and successes on:
www.facebook.com/compassionfatigue

COMPASSION FATIGUE
AWARENESS PROJECT

SECTION ONE
FOR YOU, THE CAREGIVER

This section is dedicated to you, the caregiver, with two thoughts in mind. First, that the ideas within will generate new, energizing ways to offer care. Second, that the steps will suggest ways for caregivers to practice authentic, sustainable self-care daily.

1

CREATE A SELF-CARE PLAN

When we are no longer able to change a situation, we are challenged to change ourselves. — Viktor Frankl

The best way to avoid or manage the distressing symptoms of compassion fatigue is to create a self-care plan and translate it into action every day. We now know two kinds of caregiving exist: healthy, and unhealthy or chronic. Healthy Caregiving allows us to be present to those in our care. As caregivers, we reap the positive benefits of caring for another human being. This process promotes true compassion for others while not taking on the suffering of others as our own. Unhealthy or chronic caregiving surfaces when a caregiver has not reconciled his or her own pain and suffering. The unresolved trauma can attach to the pain and suffering of others, creating an unhealthy manner of relating to those in our care. Creating and maintaining a Self-Care Plan is a sacred promise we make to ourselves to follow a plan for authentic, sustainable self-care.

First Steps

❋ Create a template for your Self-Care Plan. This life plan is for you alone or to share with trusted friends and family. It is your choice how you want to handle it.

❋ Schedule a chunk of time for yourself to reflect on your needs, values and hopes for your future. Find a place and

3

time where there are no distractions. Turn off the technology. No tweets, blogs or postings allowed during this introspective time. For your plan to be authentic to you, it must come from deep inside where all of our answers reside.

* Keep your Self-Care Plan visible. Hang it in the bathroom where you can see it first thing every morning. Post it on the refrigerator door or in your cubicle at work. Studies suggest that repeating affirmations 16 times a day can alter our brains and, ultimately, promote positive, healthy change.

* Give yourself a pat on the back when things go right. Often we take one giant step forward only to take 3 baby steps backward. Change is difficult for everyone. Think of yourself as resilient and successful. When you fall off the wagon, get back on as soon as possible. You're in for a great ride!!

* Review your Self-Care Plan regularly. Undoubtedly, it will need tweaking.

2

COMMUNICATE YOUR BOUNDARIES

We teach people how to treat us. – Dr. Phil McGraw

Creating personal boundaries means determining our limits - what we will and will not allow in our lives. When this term refers to caregiving, it takes on special meaning. To be effective, compassionate caregivers we must learn to conserve our resources and energy. In doing so, we protect ourselves from feelings of resentment, anger and fatigue. The best way to determine your personal boundaries is to assess your needs. How much alone time do you require daily to renew and refresh yourself? How much support do you need to complete the necessary caregiving tasks? If someone in your care tends to be verbally or even physically abusive, where do you draw the line?

First Steps

✳ Make a list of your top three needs. The needs can be emotional, physical or spiritual.

✳ List specific ways in which you intend to have those needs met. Intentionality means doing something with a specific outcome in mind.

✳ Be aware of the proper language to use when expressing your needs. Use terms such as "I want..." and "I need..."

Always come from a place of "I." Practice what you want to say, if necessary. Become familiar with the vocabulary.

✳ Set a time to review your personal boundaries and expectations with your person and others involved in the caregiving process.

✳ Review your progress often and make adjustments or negotiate, if necessary.

3

BE POSITIVE

Laugh and the world laughs with you. Weep and you weep alone.
– Ella Wheeler Wilcox

Scientific research shows time and again that having a positive attitude and outlook on life promotes good health and genuine gratitude, and can even attract good luck. As a caregiver, your positive energy not only affects your own well-being, but the well-being of everyone around you. We all have the ability to learn the art of being positive. Even when times get tough, we have the potential to choose between allowing the bad things to invade our thoughts and actions or encouraging hope and happiness for the future. Being positive is a coping skill that many of us may have never learned. Being positive is as easy, or difficult, as wanting to make the right choice. If we chose to be positive we reap the rewards.

First Steps

✳ Smile even when you don't feel like smiling. It brightens your face, prevents future frown wrinkles and it's infectious. A recent study from Harvard University tells us that our smiles contain a certain "infectiousness" that strongly affects others, leading the scientists to comment that "happiness is contagious."

* Start your day with a ritual that puts you in a state of positivity. This can be a relaxing hot shower, a delicious, nutritious breakfast, yoga, walking Fido or putting birdseed out for your backyard visitors. The choice is up to you.

* Refrain from reading the newspaper or turning on the morning news first thing. Unfortunately, the media creates high ratings with graphic, sensational stories and images. Don't allow television or radio stations to invade your positive private space each morning. The news can wait until you have placed positivity at the center of your being.

* Humor yourself. Is there anything that puts us in a place of feeling positive about life more than humor? If you must read the newspaper in the morning, turn to the comics and see what Snoopy is up to. If you must watch television, turn the channel to the punsters and interviewers who choose to see the world through laughing eyes.

* Keep images, cartoons, and articles in view that make you smile. We are visual people and what we look at affects us deeply. Keep a photo of a loved one who, when you look at her face, makes your heart happy. A contented, happy heart creates enough positive feelings to share with a friend or two.

4

DISCOURAGE NEGATIVITY

We are what we think, all that we are arises in our thoughts. With our thoughts, we make the world. – Buddhist tradition

Negativity saps the healing energy of a caregiver. Luckily, we each have the power within us to change our attitudes and behaviors. Becoming aware of our negativity is the first step toward positive change. Negativity can creep into the life of a caregiver without notice. Day after day, meeting the needs of another may wear thin. Feelings of anxiety, frustration, resentment and even anger can surface and lead to unhealthy caregiving practices. Once this occurs, the chances of providing a healing influence lessen and the joys associated with caregiving disappear. When a caregiver recognizes the symptoms early and administers the much-needed self-care, everyone wins. Admit that feelings of inadequacy, fatigue and confusion are often present. Creating an awareness of your situation is the first step in discouraging negativity.

First Steps

✳ Find the positive factors in your difficult and challenging situation. If you recognize the positives but have trouble keeping the negatives at bay, write out a list of positive factors and keep it where you can see it.

* Name the negative emotions that you are feeling. Can you take action to remove the negative aspects of your caregiving situation? Perhaps there is a way to come to terms with your emotions and sweep them out of your life forever.

* Keep tabs on when you feel negative most often. Is it first thing in the morning? Late in the afternoon? Does something trigger those episodes? If so, what action can you take to help manage your negative emotions? It can be something as simple as eating a healthy snack to sustain you.

* Stay away from 24/7 news shows, newspapers that thrive on chaos, magazines featuring graphic images and radio shows whose mission is to rile listeners. Find sources that lighten your mood and present life in a positive manner.

* Develop a sense of humor. Black or dark humor can bring us through some of life's most harrowing experiences. It has been said that laughter, by definition, is healthy.

* Lead by example. Smile, even when you don't feel like smiling. This proven method of encouraging others will create a more positive environment and encourage healing.

5

ENCOURAGE POSITIVE INPUT

The real art of conversation is not only to say the right thing in the right place, but to leave unsaid the wrong thing at the tempting moment.
– Dorothy Neville

Negative thoughts and feelings do nothing to aid in the healing process. As many new studies suggest, happiness is a choice. We help those in our care by modeling positive behaviors and speaking positive words. Those experiencing illness or disease often fall into a hole of negativity and depression. Life just doesn't look too promising when we see it from a pillow on a bed. As caregivers, we can go a long way in bringing cheer and lightness into the lives of those who are sick, in pain and, perhaps, suffering. We can present thoughts, ideas and activities that illicit positive response. We can bring those in our care back to a place where happiness and love were very much alive. Or we can propel them into the future where dreams take hold and keep spirits soaring. The more positive elements we can inject into a life, the more that life will feel positive.

First Steps

* Bring out the historic photos or photo album. Select the pages or photos that display happy times such as a birthday party, wedding, baptism or special anniversary. Ask questions about the people in the photo. Ask about how

he or she felt when the photo was taken. What about the clothes – what was fashionable at the time?

✳ Request that friends and family send greeting cards or short letters. Read them aloud and ask about the memories your person shares with the sender.

✳ Position your person near a window or door where the scene outside includes trees, plants, flowers, birdbaths or birdhouses. Nature heals naturally. Ask your person about his or her favorite flower, bird, or garden creature. What makes the choice a favorite?

✳ Share the feature section of the newspaper. Put aside the front section full of war, crime and deadlocked government officials. Read about dance, books, theater, and how to plant a spring vegetable garden. These themes create the positive feelings of joys in life. Keep them in the forefront.

✳ Plant a window garden full of colorful flowers. If this space isn't possible, create a planter bursting with seasonal flowers. Place it near the bedside where your person can't help but notice other living things. Talk about the seasons and which one he or she finds most memorable.

6

PROMOTE HEALTHY EATING

Eat your vegetables. – Mom

Good nutrition aids the body and mind in healing and works as a defense against further deterioration of bodily functions. Fruits, vegetables and other life-affirming nutrients hold the power to sustain life. Indulge your person's senses of sight, taste and smell by preparing high quality meals and snacks. Using local, seasonal foods also serves to connect him with the seasons of the year. There may be restrictions due to the type of illness, but for the most part, foods are adaptable. If your person is unable to digest fresh, raw foods, provide strained or stewed vegetables and fruits. If a lack of appetite is present due to a specific illness or medications, display bite-sized portions to entice him to eat at his own pace. No one enjoys eating alone. Plan your meal times to coincide with your person's. Exchange entertaining stories and be 100% present. And always remember to say a prayer of Thanksgiving before eating. There isn't a religion or spiritual practice in the world that frowns on giving thanks for the food before us.

First Steps

* Plan the menus together. Ask your person for input as to what to include in his daily diet. If you are creative on the computer, design a template for a weekly menu printout.

Make it lively, colorful and fun to look at. Include seasonal themes in your designs.

✳ Bring your person, if possible, to the local Farmer's Market to purchase fruits, vegetables and fresh flowers. The sights and sounds of a Saturday morning will remind him that life is certainly worth living no matter what the situation.

✳ Go to the library and check out books on healthy eating, slow foods and basic nutrition. Share your knowledge of the subject with your person. Determine where he can make changes to his diet that fortifies his well-being.

✳ Purchase monthly magazines that feature enticing, well-balanced meals. Have your person read the magazines and point out what appeals to him. Prepare some of the recipes that feature fresh, nutritious food. And don't forget to try a special dessert recipe, too. This activity is particularly fun and productive during the holiday season when magazines feature new and exciting ideas.

✳ Watch cooking shows on television. There is enough food preparation programming to watch a different chef or cook every day. If a recipe strikes you as interesting or tasty, be sure to write it down, whip it up and sample and critique it together.

7

ENGAGE IN THOUGHT-PROVOKING ACTIVITIES

Use it or lose it. – Unknown

Studies consistently show that we all must work tirelessly to keep our brains active. This directive also applies to those who are experiencing different stages of disease or illness. Maintaining the best possible quality of life for those we serve challenges caregivers. A person in our care may not have the energy or motivation to stay active, so it is our job as healthy caregivers to provide thought-provoking activities, even at the bedside. Jay Early, Ph. D., author of *Healing Responses and Therapeutic Change and Interactive Group Therapy*, contends, "While awareness is important and healing can emerge entirely as an internal process, healing responses from others provide a form of corrective emotional experience that is crucial to therapeutic change." Healing responses surface when presenting thought-provoking activities, soliciting responses from those in our care, and then responding in a compassionate, caring manner. This interaction is by definition, healing. Inside a human being riddled with disease there is a healthy core very much alive and well.

First Steps

* Share artwork with your person. Encourage the art of self-reflection. What does she or he think of the colors?

The images? The artist's style? What is the artist expressing?

* Devote time to the daily newspaper. Read the editorial page together. Read the Letters to the Editor. What appears to be the most pressing issue in our lives today? Does your person have an opinion she would like to share? If so, help her write a letter and email it to the editor.

* Provide puzzles – crossword and otherwise. If your person is new to crossword puzzles, be sure to provide a crossword puzzle dictionary so feelings of discouragement won't dampen the exercise.

* Read bestselling non-fiction out loud. These thought-provoking activities differ from sheer entertainment activities. Save the fun fiction for entertainment purposes, but share the non-fiction to hone a daily dose of self-reflection. Non-fiction on the best seller list often highlight historical and current day political figures, biographies and treatises on world affairs.

* Watch rousing television programming that moves the mind. Public television presents programming featuring the arts and dance. National Geographic takes us to places unknown. Even the food network can take us away from our everyday worries and into a world of foreign foods and their preparation.

8

KEEP UP ON CURRENT EVENTS

When vividly aware through some particular sense, keep in the awareness.
– Sanskrit movement

Maintaining an awareness of what's happening in your neighborhood, your city, your state, your country and your world reaps positive benefits for both you and those in your care. When your person is confined to a limited space, the world can appear very small. This perception aids in negative thinking, poor self-care practices, inability to be resilient in the face of illness and can even lead to a lack of hope for the future. This is especially true for someone who lived a life full of curiosity, excitement and passion. In order to bring those elements back, caregivers must create an environment where discussion, opinion and increased knowledge are still the norm. The ways in which to accomplish this task are numerous given the multimedia choices we all have at our fingertips today. Below are five ways in which to stir up interest, introduce new ideas and share in the joy of knowing that every person alive, no matter what his circumstance, has the ability to make a difference.

First Steps

* Subscribe to several newspapers. This array of periodicals can range from a big city daily such as the New York Times or the Washington Post, to the weekly newspaper

published free of charge in your town or city. Read the newspapers together, sharing stories that resonate with you.

✳ Join an online political website. It doesn't matter what the political leanings might be. Elections routinely occur both at the national, state and local levels. Stay in touch with what's happening and discuss similar or differing views. Allow those in your care to be the solution, whether that means sending a donation to a political campaign, signing a petition or writing a letter to your representatives.

✳ Watch documentaries. There are countless documentaries now available on myriad subjects. Rent, purchase or record documentaries as a way to encourage new thoughts and perceptions. Hook in to historical subjects that interest your person such as World War II. Watching a film on the Battle of the Bulge could conjure up memories for discussion.

✳ Read books aloud. The list of best sellers concerning topics of national and international interest is endless. Discover a favorite author, such as Pulitzer Prize-winning writer Doris Kearns Goodwin, and read all of her books. Compare subject matter, photos and writing style.

✳ Check television listings for interesting programs that educate and entertain such as the History Channel. Mindless television shows do nothing to encourage wellness and squelch the impulse to want to make a difference.

9

LEARN & IMPLEMENT PAIN MANAGEMENT TECHNIQUES

To be alive at all is to have scars. — John Steinbeck

Lessening pain creates a better world for both the person and the caregiver. When pain is present, a person experiences not only physical ailments, but emotional and spiritual ailments as well. With chronic pain, an ordinarily kind, caring person can become irritable, restless and demanding. By learning and implementing pain management techniques, a caregiver can help to both regulate and manage the amount of pain the person is feeling. Many of the techniques require household items and are easily administered. Watching someone in pain can be excruciating. As caregivers, we often feel powerless to stop the pain or at least express sympathy for the person and his or her situation. The good news is that we don't have to be caregivers to administer a number of simple strategies that reduce pain through relaxation methods, music, controlled breathing, and distraction. Below are some ideas to utilize when needed.

First Steps

❋ Massage – Apply a rubbing motion to a shoulder, a hand or a foot can relieve pain. This process also encourages support and respect between person and caregiver. Massage heals both the giver and the receiver.

✳ Play Music – Recent studies show that music taps into our pleasure centers. Ask your person if she prefers classical, jazz, popular, Broadway hits or a Latin beat. While you may prefer classical, be sure to follow through on your person's choice. Beethoven's Fifth may settle you down, but the strength of his minor notes may distress your person.

✳ Relax – Relieve muscle tension by quieting the environment, moderating deep, down in the diaphragm, breathing, and creating a relaxing scene through verbal narration. Don't forget to add the warm, healing sunshine, gentle lapping waves, and refreshing light winds.

✳ Position - Posture your person often so his body maintains and promotes comfortable muscle and bones function. Use movement as a way of keeping joints and ligaments pliable.

✳ Employ distractions – Allow Fido to interact with your person. Bring out the memory album and ask questions about the people and places depicted in the photographs.

10

INSERT HUMOR INTO EVERY DAY

Laughter, by definition, is healthy. – Doris Lessing

It's often difficult to find humor in situations where a loved one is in pain and suffering. It can feel irreverent to laugh when someone is crying. But the truth is that, as caregivers, we must find balance in our lives every day in order to keep providing healthy care to others. And one way to assure that happens is through humor. You may feel as if your smile is lost forever, but it's not. It's still there waiting to savor the little things that make life worthwhile.

First Steps

* Relax with your person. Caregiving is stressful. Often we can't see the small treasures around us when we are mired in sadness. Taking a deep breath and realizing that pain is a "normal" part of life will help you to relax. When we are mindful of the world around us, we are more open to what is occurring on many levels. Develop an awareness of the hidden moments that hold the precious gift of time. Look around and you will find someone who wants to provide a giggle or two. Children and animals are great at this.

* Build balance into your life every day. If you see pain and suffering every day, all day, you are bound to see life as a downer. There will be the high points and the low points. Be sure to embrace the high points. Spend time with friends and loved ones who make you laugh.

✳ Allow others to help. Old segments of *Fraser*, *Seinfeld* and even as far back as *I Love Lucy* can help you find your smile again. Jim Carrey does a good job of it, too. Bring these comedians into your home and let them entertain you.

✳ Tell silly jokes. (Even knock, knock jokes will suffice.) The sillier, the better. Here's one to get you started:

Q: How do you get a handkerchief to dance?

A: You put a little boogie in it!

✳ Laugh with your person. The human body offers myriad avenues to humor with its weird noises and quirks. Walk along those paths and find humor in being human.

11

CHANGE YOUR ENVIRONMENT REGULARLY

If nothing changes, nothing changes. – Unknown

Altering the person's environment allows him or her to refresh and see life from a new perspective. Can replacing a vase of summer daisies with a vase of fall chrysanthemums aid in healing? Definitely, yes! Human beings are deeply affected by what goes on around them. Even the most unaware people will admit that the weather, what they read in the morning newspaper, or what's happening in their neighborhood does carry some weight in how they view their world. This is especially true of those who are ill or confined to a small space such as a bedroom, hospital room or even a wheelchair. It is possible for a recovering person who has access to an entire house to feel confined, especially if she lived a very active life. Keep those in your care aware of the immediate world around them as well as the larger world, in which they continue to be active members.

First Steps

✳ Awaken the senses with flowers. Change arrangements often and pay particular attention to color choices and seasonal selections. We are all coded to the seasons of our lives. Make sure the flowers do not emit a strong fragrance. Mild is always better. If allergies are present, alternate houseplants.

* Create a photo display of your person's loved ones. Don't forget to include beloved pets and favored sights, such as vacation spots visited or cities of origin. Digital frames work perfectly as you can program hundreds of photographs which will loop automatically. Enjoying these photos will spark memories which in turn keep the brain active and stimulated. They also serve as catalysts for memories to share.

* Encourage family and friends to bring colorful, life-affirming gifts such as bright balloons and stuffed animals. There are delightful ways to keep your person engaged with life.

* Invite children related to the person to paint, draw or color large murals to hang on the walls or a bulletin board. Children have a way of transforming the most depressing situations into ones of hope and laughter.

* Welcome the seasons. Colorful flowers in the spring; pumpkins in the fall go a long way to lighten the load. Include a plate of seasonal treats bedside. While appetites might wane during illness, who can resist a merrily decorated holiday cookie? If cost is an issue, take a walk outside and bring some of nature's beauty indoors. Autumn leaves bunched in a vase or pinecones placed in a basket can cheer even the most unhappy person.

12

BE A GOOD LISTENER

The most important trip you can take is to meet others halfway.
– Henry Boye

There is a huge difference between listening and hearing. As caregivers, we often believe we know what is best for those in our care. While it may be true some of the time, it is not always true. Nothing impinges on healing more than sensing we are not being heard. Through our words, we proclaim who we are, what we expect, what we need, and most important, how we choose to live out our lives. To excel in the fine art of listening, we must not only listen with our ears, we must listen with our hearts.

First Steps

* Ask. If there is one action that creates good communication, it is to ask someone a well-placed question…and then wait until you have heard the answer. Something as simple as asking if your person prefers apple juice to grape juice ensures a healthy connection. Giving someone a choice says that you care.

* Develop good listening skills. The first skill is very simple: act like a good listener. Put all of your attention on your person. You are a better listener when you look directly at

your person. Making eye contact is the best way to let the other person know he or she has your full attention.

❋ Play back what you thought you heard if you feel you don't understand an answer to your question. Give your person a chance to further explain his or her needs. If you still don't understand, continue using different words until you both agree that comprehensive communication has occurred.

❋ React to what your person is saying. Nod, smile, touch a shoulder – provide any action that shows you are listening, hearing and are reacting to what he or she has to say.

❋ Follow through on any promises you have made during the course of the communication. This interaction builds trust and a connection that will aid in the healing process.

13

BE A CAREGIVER'S ADVOCATE

One person can make a difference and every person should try.
– John Fitzgerald Kennedy

President Kennedy understood the power of one. As caregivers, we are often overwhelmed with our tasks at hand. Every minute counts when providing care to another human being. But what many caregivers don't know is that taking on the role of an advocate can re-energize and revitalize our caregiving mission. Finding time to voice an opinion via an email, tweet or blog can go far in supporting a caregiving cause or changing a law. With health care reform in a tenuous state, it is all the more important to take a stand. It may be about caregiver's rights, or challenges inherent in staffing, or how to deal with compassion fatigue on the job. Additionally, caregivers are empowered to speak up for those who either don't believe they have a voice or are truly unable to speak for themselves.

First Steps

✳ Join a network that supports your caregiving cause. Sign on to an advocacy website to receive updates and opportunities to speak out in favor of your caregiving issues.

✳ Participate in web alerts calling for support on legislation. If nothing else, take a stand against our government cutting funding for health care. Become acquainted with your local, state and national legislators. Learn how they vote on issues affecting health care.

* Share your passion for caregiving with friends and neighbors. Make them aware of how your legislators are voting. Ask for their support in helping to make a difference. If they can't spare the time, ask for financial support.

* Register for a caregiving webinar or course at your community college. Not only will you learn more about the issues that interest you, you can also network with others who believe as you do.

* Start your own caregiving advocacy program. If none of the opportunities speak to you, create a plan to educate others about caregiving, its challenges and rewards. Present a workshop at your local hospital, church or community organization. Before you know it, the power of one will become the power of many.

14

BE AWARE OF RELIGIOUS AND SPIRITUAL PRACTICES

My religion is kindness. – Dalai Lama

Healthy caregiving begins and ends with a heartfelt respect for the religious/spiritual beliefs of others. There are as many religious and spiritual beliefs today as there are people roaming the earth. If you don't know which one(s) apply to your person – ask. Studies show that religious rituals and spiritual behaviors add a high level of comfort that can't be found in any other human interactions. As the caregiver, you may be asked to fulfill religious or spiritual needs. This may be something as simple as scheduling a home visit with a local pastor or creating a bedside altar. Either way, creating a spiritual realm for your person will be a positive force in the healing process.

First Steps

* Go to the library or local bookstore and find one or two books that offer comforting readings. Some books suggest "food for thought" which could open up some solid communication between you and your person.

* Spend some time researching rituals and practices. Feel free to ask your person questions about his or her beliefs. These kinds of conversations can lead to end-of-the-care decisions that are much needed in many situations.

29

✽ Purchase a spiritual item for your person that resonates with his or her religion or spirituality – prayer beads, a rosary bracelet or statuette of a favorite saint or spiritual icon.

✽ Invite a Eucharistic minister onsite to distribute Holy Communion. Receiving Holy Communion daily can be of the utmost importance to someone practicing this religion. Schedule a special blessing for your person. Every faith community recognizes the sick and suffering and in some way expresses hope and healing in a blessing or ritual.

✽ Create an altar containing icons from your person's particular tradition. If flowers are acceptable, bring fresh, seasonal flowers in on a regular basis.

15

APPLY THE DYNAMICS OF HEALTHY CAREGIVING

Peace comes from within. Do not seek it without. – Buddha

Healthy caregiving consists of tending to the whole person: body, mind and spirit. Humans have evolved into a culture of curing. When, indeed, we need to also create a culture of caring. Treating all aspects of the human condition, which includes the body, the mind and the spirit, will benefit the whole person no matter what his or her physical, mental or medical condition. Your person will reap the benefits of feeling healthier physically, emotionally, mentally and spiritually. The object of this type of healthy caregiving is to bring your person back to wholeness and in the presence of peace. It is a simple process of working with your person to understand and accept that he or she still has control of life decisions and can still affect the world around them. It is empowering and life-affirming.

First Steps

❋ Allow a healthy expression of emotions. It isn't always easy to listen to a person who is experiencing pain and suffering. But in order to promote holistic healing, we must accept that your person will express a whole gamut of human emotions. And it is okay.

✻ Know how to calm your person when he or she becomes anxious, nervous, frightened or sad. This not only includes calming the mind, but the body as well. Use techniques that are known to calm such as massage and soothing music.

✻ Work with your person to expand inner resources that strengthen and heal. These exercises could include prayer, meditation, reading poetry or bible passages. These inner resources can be called upon to be able to deal with whatever life has in store.

✻ Provide situations where your person can acknowledge and respond to the healthy relationships in his or her life. Guide the interactions in a manner that are positive, where good thoughts and feelings are expressed.

✻ Help your person to understand that maintaining a higher quality of life is a goal if he or she exhibits unhealthy behaviors or habits such as smoking, excessive alcohol consumption or overeating. Even those who are terminally ill and still able to function on a certain level will reap the benefits of healthy choices.

16

UNDERSTAND YOUR PERSON'S AILMENT OR DISEASE

No one cares how much you know until they know how much you care.
– Unknown

The caregiver must fully understand the nature of any illnesses, the treatments being received and any emergency procedures to be followed should the person's condition worsen. Always be observant. Signs of a condition getting worse, or even better, must never go unnoticed. Another area of responsibility for the caregiver is to the family or friends of the person receiving care. These people are trusting you with the well being of a dearly loved friend/relative. Always be sure to keep them notified.

First Steps

✳ Understand how people feel and express pain differently. Pain is an important indicator in illness and disease. Apply a measurement technique such as 1 being little or no pain and 10 being extreme pain.

✳ Learn about the disease or illness of your person and put special emphasis on understanding and the ability to recognize symptoms.

✳ Stay up to date on your person's illness or disease. Read journals, publications and other documents explaining the latest studies, procedures and processes.

✳ Embrace a holistic approach to illness. Consider factors outside the biological process such as emotional and psychological landscape of your person.

✳ Treat the person – body, mind, and spirit – along with the disease or illness.

17

KNOW EMERGENCY PROCEDURES

When in doubt, call 911. – Anonymous

In order to successfully weather a caregiving emergency, it is imperative that a caregiver has a clear knowledge of medical emergency procedures and information. Advanced preparation is the best gift you can give yourself. A calm demeanor during an emergency is imperative to process the most profound emergency with a minimum of drama and chaos. Unexpected emergencies, whether produced from the outside such as a power outage or an earthquake or directly from the person's medical condition, call for a "take charge" personality. As a caregiver, there is arguably nothing you can do that better equips you to care for others than to know how to execute emergency procedures. Along with knowing CPR, first aid, and the Heimlich maneuver, it is necessary to know your community and where key facilities are located. Remember that remaining calm, collected and organized will serve your person and his or her family members best. This collective knowledge will empower you to take the lead and instill the self-confidence that is necessary to get you through any emergency situation as quickly as it arises.

First Steps

* Know where your local hospital Emergency Room is located and where to park your car when delivering someone

in an emergency situation. If possible, take a tour of the facility.

✳ Educate yourself as to life-threatening symptoms such as chest pains, severe abdominal pain, seizures, sudden dizziness, weakness or loss of coordination or balance, sudden blurred vision, and coughing up or vomiting blood. Keep a medical first aid manual in a handy place.

✳ Educate yourself about non-life threatening emergencies that need immediate attention such as allergic reactions, insect bite reactions, sprains and strains, upper respiratory infections, and urinary tract infections.

✳ Place an up-to-date, well-stocked First Aid Kit within reaching distance. Check the supplies often to be sure they haven't been depleted.

✳ Keep emergency information in one place. This packet should include: phone numbers of police, fire, hospital and paramedics. Personal information concerning the person should include: insurance card, list of medications, list of allergies to medications, emergency contact list, advanced directives and organ donation forms, as well as a written medical history.

18

PREPARE FOR AN EMERGENCY

Nothing in life is to be feared, it is only to be understood.
— Madame Curie

Anticipating emergencies is not the same as anxiously awaiting for an emergency to surface. When one is amply prepared, he can rest assured that he can react as quickly and safely as possible in a time of need. Taking the time to prepare yourself and your environment for an unexpected emergency can save lives. Once you understand the need for prior preparation, it is a matter of organizing time to study or take courses, purchase the supplies necessary to survive comfortably, and most important, prepare those in your care and perhaps your colleagues how to best react should an emergency occur. It is never a waste of time to hold emergency drills. This applies not only to medical facilities and elder care facilities, but also private homes.

First Steps

‡ Water is the first basic of survival. It is recommended that one gallon per day per person is stored in a cool, safe place. Check the label for storage longevity and be sure to replace outdated supplies. If the storage time is out-dated and drinking is prohibited, use the water on lawns, plants, or birdbaths.

✻ Food is the second basic of survival. A three-day supply of non-perishable food per person should also be stored in an appropriate area. Keep packaged foods in secure storage bags to avoid dampness. Try to pack a variety of foods in cans, jars, and singly wrapped. Take dietary needs of your person into consideration when selecting types of foods. Be sure to include a can opener when storing the food. Check for dates and restock, when necessary. If you have too much food to discharge, consider taking it to a soup kitchen or homeless shelter.

✻ Warmth is the third basic of survival. Store an ample supply of blankets, sleeping bags, or quilts in a dry, safe storage area. If space allows, include pillows and possibly blow-up mattresses to provide comfort for your person.

✻ Prepare emergency supplies for house pets. Again, store enough dry and canned food for at least three days. Pets also need water to survive, so include a bowl to hold the water. Knowing a beloved pet is cared for during an emergency will help lower the stress level of those in your care.

✻ Store the following necessary emergency items: battery-powered and hand-crank radios, NOAA weather radio, extra batteries, flashlights, moist towelettes, garbage bags and plastic ties for sanitation needs and toilet paper.

19

SPEARHEAD INJURY PREVENTION

I hear and I forget. I see and I remember. I do and I understand.
– Confucius

There is more to taking care of another person than administering medications, preventing bed sores and being a helpful companion. In order to protect your person and yourself, a caregiver needs to take the lead and be sure the surrounding environment is safe for everyone. Injuries from a fall can sideline a person faster than a disease. This is particularly true with the elderly in our care. Fragile bones break easily; fragile psyches break even easier. Stories abound about patients on the mend who take a fall only to go downhill mentally, physically, emotionally and spiritually. Many never recover. These accidents can be prevented and we caregivers can go a long way toward making an environment safe, for not only those who are ill, but for ourselves as well.

First Steps

* Assess the area where you are providing care. This may be an apartment, a house, a mobile home or within your organization. Pay attention to accidents waiting to happen, especially in the bathroom where most injuries occur.

* Make a shopping list of items that need to be purchased in order to create a safer environment (i.e., stepstools

without wheels, handles to make getting in and out of the tub or shower safer, medical alert system, etc.). Go buy or order what is needed or contact an organization that offers installation of safety devices.

✳ Explain to your person what you are planning to do. Describe the items and how they will lessen the chances of an unfortunate accident.

✳ Install all of the safety items or services according to directions. If you have trouble understanding the instructions to install items properly, call in a handyperson.

✳ Put the newly installed items to good use. That one time when you bypass the safety feature is the time someone is going to get injured. Keep a log of the days that pass without any injuries or accidents and share the good news with those in your care.

20

FALL-PROOF YOUR CAREGIVING AREA

Let us not look back in anger or forward in fear, but around in awareness. – James Thurber

One in three people over age 65 fall annually. Most of the time, the fall occurs in their own home, apartment or condo. Serious injuries, such as a hip fracture, greatly increase the chance of an early death. Thinking ahead and preparing your caregiving area can help prevent falls and injuries. Studies show that up to 30% of adults over age 65 suffer serious repercussions following a fall. These types of injuries can take weeks and months to heal, if at all. The after effects often create issues such as an inability to get around easily or to move without pain. Fall-proofing your area goes a long way toward keeping those in your care safe and healthy.

First Steps

❋ Install grab bars on bathroom and bedroom walls. This is especially necessary in the bathroom near the toilet, shower and bathtub.

❋ Purchase a number of night lights and place them throughout the area. Make sure the lights create a path to and from the bathroom, where most accidents can occur.

✳ Check the entire area for loose wires and cords. If they can't be removed, purchase a roll of colorful duck tape and tape them to the floor so they are visible and easily seen.

✳ Take inventory of all of the rugs, carpets and bathroom mats. Are they secured to the floor? If not, tack all carpets down, place nonskid rubber mats in the shower stall and in the bathtub. Don't forget to check the mats in the kitchen as well. Make sure kitchen mats are non-skid and tape them down for double assurance.

✳ Place hairbrushes, cosmetics, cotton balls, toothpaste, etc., in a basket on the bathroom counter for easy access. This also keeps your area neat and tidy. If your person is able to make coffee or use the toaster, be sure all appliances are easily within reach. This goes for bathroom items too, such as hairdryers, toothbrushes and other grooming items.

✳ Teach your person how to use a cell phone or alert system. So if a fall occurs, a call to 911 immediately following an incident can save a life.

21

PRAY OR MEDITATE

There is a moment in every day that the devil cannot find. — Unknown

Prayer or meditation can be as simple as sitting quietly looking out a bedroom window. When caregivers take time to be quiet and listen, we hear our inner voice guiding us to be still and find inner peace. Prayer or meditation delivers comfort and strength during difficult times. This is not only true for a person suffering or in pain, but also for the caregiver who tends to his or her needs during this time. The acts of prayer or meditation are highly personal and help us to connect with ourselves and others on a deeper level. There is no right or wrong path to prayer. Much like self-care, what works best is what is authentic and sustainable to the person. If you haven't yet discovered your prayer or meditation ritual that calms and relaxes you, don't despair. Learning to pray or mediate is a process. Here are some steps to help.

First Steps

* Take as much time as you need to erase all preconceptions of what you believe prayer or meditation is and what will be accomplished. The best way to begin this process is with a clean slate.

* Entertain simple rituals such as taking time before a meal to stop and take a deep breath. Connect with the gratefulness

and thankfulness you feel that you have food before you. The simplest way to tap into the well of spirituality that lives in each of us is to practice daily rituals.

✳ Jumpstart your prayer or meditation practice by enjoying nature. Find a spot that appeals to your senses. Is it the seashore? The mountains? In a forest? Or maybe it's right in your own backyard. Find ten minutes in your busy day to let the beauty of nature engulf you. Be still.

✳ Trust in your prayers or the power of meditation. Keep a prayer journal. Review it regularly and see how prayer is working in your life. Delightful surprises are in store.

✳ Share prayer or meditation practices with others, especially those in your care. As time goes on, you will find great power in prayer and meditation. The positive outcomes increase exponentially when we pray or meditate together. Continue to build a diverse and peace-filled prayer or meditation life.

SECTION TWO
FOR THOSE IN YOUR CARE

Section Two is for your person, as well as his or her family and friends. The ideas within this section are to bring loved ones together to create an environment of help, hope and healing.

22

ENCOURAGE GOOD GROOMING PRACTICES

To love oneself is the beginning of a lifelong romance. – Oscar Wilde

Something as simple as a haircut, facial or manicure can lift spirits and promote wellbeing. Whether your person is highly mobile or completely bedridden, he or she will thrive when you offer a spa treatment of any kind. You don't have to be a licensed cosmetologist to trim a beard or polish nails. Most good grooming skills improve with practice. Your person might be too embarrassed to ask for help with nail clipping or a shave, so ask.

First Steps

✳ Create an attractive basket of grooming supplies. Include the basics such as haircutting scissors, nail clippers, deodorant and hair curlers. Go to discount stores such as Wal-Mart or Target to get good bargains. Add colorful nail polishes, lipsticks and fun facial masques to entice your person to give good grooming a try. And remember, spa days are not only for women, men enjoy pampering, too.

✳ Start with a small gesture if your person is reluctant to be touched or fussed over. A haircut trim or eyebrow pluck are good for starters. Enjoy beauty magazines such as Elle, GQ, More or Ladies Home Journal. Perusing these magazines will, hopefully, spark an interest in self-care grooming and perhaps a grooming improvement project.

* Set up regular appointments for haircuts, manicures, or pedicures if your person is mobile. This will give your person something to anticipate. Believe it or not, some beauticians will make house calls!

* Splurge on a quality hand-held mirror. Keep it by the bedside or somewhere handy and convenient where your person can enjoy the fruits of the labor.

* Compliment your person on a regular basis. There is no sin in taking pride in one's appearance. Offer uplifting, positive comments daily.

Note: A suggested list of Spa Basket items can be found in the Resource section at the back of this book.

23

TEACH TECHNOLOGY

It's not a faith in technology. It's faith in people. – Steve Jobs

Keep your person well connected. Chances are good your person is a Baby Boomer or older. Technology is not second nature to these generations. Computers can appear foreign, iPhones are a mystery, and Kindles are of no use. Often this dread of technology stems from a lack of understanding and training. They are missing out on the tremendous benefits these machines can provide. Caregivers can make an enormous difference in the lives of their persons by opening the door to technology.

First Steps

✳ Share Facebook, Twitter, and Skype capabilities with your person. Explain how you keep in close touch with family and friends even though you live miles and miles apart. Explain how they, too, can be hooked into their loved ones.

✳ Start with a simple plan by paving a path to success. Ask your person who he or she would like to connect with regularly. The easiest first step is most likely learning to use email. Show your person how simple it is to send and receive emails. Write the directions down by hand and keep them close for easy reference. The fear of technology is very real to those who didn't grow up texting and tweeting.

* Use a simple video camera or smartphone to record a message from your person to a loved one and post it on You Tube. Contact family and friends of your person and send the link. Create brief videos regularly and share them. This is especially charming when grandchildren are involved.

* Create a hard copy log of all emails, links and websites that interest your person. He or she can refer to this list when you are not onsite to assist them.

* Continue to build a repertoire of communication outlets for your person. Using technology to stay connected will create a sense of happiness, efficiency and a healthy outlook on life.

Note: Purchase the simplest technology possible such as the Kindle to download books. Too many outlets and gadgets will only confuse and frustrate first time users. Keep it simple.

24

MAKE MUSIC A PART OF EVERY DAY

Without music, life is a journey through a desert. – Pat Conroy

It has been known for many years that music soothes the soul and heals the human body. More recently, neuroscientists are delving further into the research and finding that music can actually rewire our brains and jumpstart healing mechanisms. In the field of music therapy, professionals are now certified to work in hospitals, nursing homes, special needs classrooms and rehabilitation centers to help stimulate the development or recovery of functions lost to illness or injury. Neuroscientists are focusing on types of musical improvisations and techniques that work best for certain disabilities, and caregivers can hook into this vital research and create musical treatments to soothe and relax their persons. Music components such as harmony, melody and rhythm engage different portions of the brain where speech, movement and social interactions originate.

First Steps

* Prepare a program of several different types of music to present to your person. Allow your person to make the final selections for your weekly program. If your person exhibits a high level of musical savvy, just jot down his or her favorites and download the music.

* Select the best mechanism for delivering the music, depending on the condition and requirements of your person. If your person is bed-ridden, perhaps a stereo or radio might work best. If your person is able to be up and around, an iPod with comfortable ear pods allows mobility.

* Forget the iPod and sing! Studies show that persons with impaired speech respond well to singing simple melodies. The rhythm of singing serves to improve the fluency of speech. This is especially true of stroke and stuttering persons.

* Clap your hands if you're happy and you know it. It could help. Ask your person to tap her foot or drum her fingers in time to the music. These movements are known to stimulate brain function. Forget Tony Bennett and put on a John Phillip Souza march.

* Go for a walk and have your person maintain a steady, rhythmic stride to music with a distinct, heavy beat. This exercise will help with balance, steadiness and movement.

25

PROVIDE COMFORTABLE BEDDING

The bed has become a place of luxury to me! I would not exchange it for all the thrones in the world. — Napoleon Bonaparte

Your person may not feel the same way as Napoleon Bonaparte about his bed. But if he is bed-ridden or in need of bed rest, the least a caregiver can do is make it as comfortable as possible. This task not only includes selecting the appropriate bed, but also researching different kinds of mattresses, pads, sheets, pillows and blankets. Luckily, prices range from ultra-expensive to completely reasonable. Don't forget to add colors and design into the mix.

First Steps

❋ Discuss the bed situation with your person's physician. If your person needs an adjustable hospital bed you need to know some are manually adjusted and some are adjusted electrically. Do your research before you are ready to purchase or rent.

❋ Contact the insurance company and/or Medicare to ask if they cover the costs. Chances are good that they do, but the prescription must come through a physician and a "Certificate of Medical Necessity" must also be filled out.

✳ Locate a reputable medical supply company and ask questions. Do they cover periodic maintenance or repairs if you need to keep the bed long term? What other supplies do they offer? Mattresses? Waterproof mattress pads? Absorbent sheets? Perhaps a wheelchair or walker also, if necessary.

✳ Select non-porous fabric if your person requires antiallergic materials. Since this kind of fabric doesn't breathe, it may be too warm. Microfiber polyester fabrics or tightly woven cottons will provide comfort, but may make for a hot sleeping environment. Instead, consider a microfiber polyester fabric, a cotton fabric with a laminated nylon membrane, or a cotton fabric tightly woven with very fine threads.

✳ Make sure the bedding you buy fully encases the entire bed, including the mattress and box spring, plus protectors for all your pillows. There are even brands that carry coverings for your comforters.

26

SCREEN VISITORS

Never miss an opportunity to make others happy, even if you have to leave them alone in order to do so. – Unknown

Well-received visitors can lift the spirits and the healing energy of those in your care. Before any positive healing effects can take place you, the caregiver, must determine whether or not certain visitors are truly welcome. On the whole, it is always best to keep visitors to a minimum if not just due to transferring germs to someone who is ill. This is especially true of children and teenagers who often overlook simple symptoms such as a runny nose, a slight sore throat or a vague stomachache. There are ways to determine your person's true feelings about a possible visitor. Watching for body language, facial expressions and hidden meanings in their wording can lead you to discover the true relationship and whether or not a certain person will be helpful in the healing process.

First Steps

✽ Ask your person. Caregivers certainly don't want to find themselves in the middle of family dysfunction. Asking questions pertaining to family members could feel very uncomfortable. The same is true of neighbors who appear helpful or work colleagues who stop by unexpectedly. Best to begin the process by asking the person in your care if there are certain people s/he doesn't wish to see.

✳ Honor the answer. That nice little neighbor Rosie down the street seems so sweet and caring. But for some reason, your person refuses to be in the same room as Rosie. Trust her judgment and offer Rosie a kind word and send her on her way. Looks can be, and often are, deceiving. Best not to upset your person and gain her trust by being loyal.

✳ Make a list. Take the time to create a "Visitor's List" with your person. This will give her time to think about who she wants to see, and when. Often with long-term illnesses, persons feel alone and abandoned. These natural feelings are not reason enough to allow someone access to the person's inner sanctum. Myriad feelings surface during an illness. Some as simple as vanity; others as deep seated as anger or resentment for someone and her past actions. Either way, the person's feelings need to be validated.

✳ Help visitors feel special by preparing a snack and beverage. Guests can feel awkward in a situation where a family member or friend is ill or bed-ridden. Keep visits short, but let them know they are welcome to return.

✳ Prepare a Guest Book for guests who are welcome to sign in and leave a message behind. These notes can serve as an emotional booster at any time when your person needs a pick me up.

27

TAKE A HIKE

It is impossible to walk rapidly and be unhappy. – Mother Theresa

You may not be able to walk rapidly with your person, but even a slow, relaxing walk can soothe nerves, lift spirits and promote wellness. The benefits of taking a walk, or a hike as we call it, are plentiful. Aside from the psychological richness that comes from being outdoors, there are myriad physiological rewards. Putting one foot in front of the other, swinging our arms, and breathing deeply are known to lower blood pressure, aid in digestion and keep arthritis at bay. If your person is able to walk briskly, add to the pleasure by attaching a pedometer to keep track of how far you travel. This action can be a motivator. If your person isn't able to walk briskly or in some cases at all, use a cane, a walker or a wheelchair. Any means that propels you outdoors and into fresh air benefits both person and caregiver. And do it on a regular basis. Make time every day for a hike, weather permitting.

First Steps

* Stay close to your person and don't allow him or her to be left alone anytime before, during or after your hike.

* Keep tabs on the weather. If it looks like there is a chance of rain, plan ahead. Bring wet weather gear – water repellent jacket and umbrella.

＊ Pack water and light snacks if your person is able to hike a distance. Trail mix and fresh fruit are easy to pack and always delicious and energy producing.

＊ Layer clothes. This is especially true of your person. Elderly persons can experience chills even in warm weather. Lightweight windbreakers are best as the top layer.

＊ Wear comfortable shoes. If you or your person experience blistering, clean the area, apply the appropriate salve and cover the injury. Keep an eye on the spot to ensure proper healing.

28

INTRODUCE ANIMAL-ASSISTED THERAPY

One of the most fundamental advantages of animal assisted therapy over other therapeutic modalities is that it provides the patient a much-needed opportunity to give affection as well as receive it. It is this reciprocity - rare among medical therapies - that makes AAT a unique and valuable route to healing. – Dr. Andrew Weil

We know our furry friends provide companionship, friendship and loyalty. We also know they hold the power to aid in healing. Animals of all kinds have been properly trained in the rigors of assisting in the healing process. The right match between human and animal can improve the physical, social, emotional functions of your person. Dogs, cats, lizards, elephants, goats, birds, rabbits and horses are some of the animals used in animal assisted therapy and are referred to as comfort animals.

First Steps

* Ask permission to bring an animal into the caregiving arena. Bring a dog, cat or other therapy animal into a situation where your person isn't properly prepared and you may lose the trust that is always needed to provide healthy caregiving.

* Do your homework once you have received approval for animal assisted therapy or activities. Many people think a well-behaved animal is enough to offer their pet as a

therapy animal. This couldn't be further from the truth. Therapy animals are highly trained and have specific characteristics designed to improve many aspects of your person's life. Read more at the Delta Society website. They are the leaders in this field. Go to www.deltasociety.com.

✳ Understand the difference between therapy animals and service animals. The latter are animals that assist persons with disabilities by providing emotional and physical support. Service animals live with their humans and are trained to fulfill specific needs. Most likely, what you want is an animal trained in providing physical and emotional comfort, usually for a certain period of time each week.

✳ Discern what benefit your person will derive from animal-assisted therapy. These highly-trained animals can provide motivational, educational and recreational interactions with your person. Children have been known to improve their reading skills by reading to a therapy animal trained in this area. How will your person's quality of life be enhanced with a visit from one of these amazing animals?

✳ Educate yourself about this ever-changing field of animal-assisted therapy and activities. One of the best sources is the American Humane website at www.americanhumane.org. It's a great place to start.

29

ENCOURAGE CREATIVE ACTIVITIES

Inspiration usually comes during work, rather than before it.
– Madeleine L'Engle

Human beings are inherently creative. This gift flourishes when focused on projects that energize the spirit and hold interest. This is especially true when we create something that enhances the quality of life – for ourselves and others. As caregivers, our days are usually filled with activities we must do as opposed to activities we want to do. As the person in need of care, her days are filled with doctor appointments, medications and worries about the future. A creative project, particularly when accomplished together, can bring joy and satisfaction, and most important, ensure a healing environment.

First Steps

* Talk to your person about his or her interests. If the response is negative, do not let that hinder your next step, which is to do some research. If your person doesn't offer input, make an informed decision (take a good guess what he or she may enjoy).

* Go to the library, bookstore, local hobby shop or stationary store to find out what supplies are available.

✳ Keep your projects simple and inexpensive. If there is a chance the project is not successful or doesn't turn out as expected, no one will feel disappointed.

✳ Create a schedule to work on the project together. Special time needs to be set aside to share expertise and ideas.

✳ Be prepared to be a cheerleader if things don't go as planned. Encourage, support and praise your person. Let the project morph into something else, if necessary.

✳ Build a birdhouse, paint a paint-by-number picture, work a complex jigsaw puzzle, build a model airplane, create a recipe and bake a pie from scratch, write a poem, or sew a quilt. The ideas are endless.

30
TEACH THE ART OF JOURNALING

I have never traveled without my diary. One should always have something sensational to read on the train. – Oscar Wilde

The health benefits of journaling have been understood for a long time. Putting pen to paper is the easiest way to clean out your head. Take what's inside and put it down on paper outside as a means of releasing stress, worry and indecision. This process also clarifies thoughts and feelings, and helps the writer become self-acquainted. Journaling can be an extremely powerful tool for self-care and healing. Journal with your person and you both win.

First Steps

* Purchase 3 or 4 journals. Make sure the images or design on the outside are appealing to you and your person. You will spend some time each day with this diary, so you will not want to tire of seeing it.

* Decide together on what time of each day you will take time to write down your thoughts, feelings and whatever else surfaces. You get to make the rules. Spend 10 minutes or 30 minutes, it's up to you to decide.

* Start with a quote, a short story or a reading that gets the creative juices flowing. Choose an object that stirs up a

memory, perhaps a photo, a pressed flower, or a piece of jewelry.

✳ Forget punctuation and spelling when writing. It is more important to unleash the thoughts than to stop to be sure you are spelling a word correctly. Many people use the "stream of consciousness" method wherein no filter is applied. This method can be very useful if anger or hostility are present.

✳ Share your writings. Or not. It's all up to you and your person. Your journal can remain under lock and key, or it can be open for the whole world to see.

31

DESIGN A MEMORY ALBUM

God gives us certain memories so we may have roses in December.
– Unknown

A memory album can include anything from photographs to greeting cards to diplomas. It is a gathering spot for treasures of the heart. You may need to include family members in order to locate enough items to create a substantial life memory collection. If you find your person hasn't hoarded his or her life treasures into one place, you may need to call on others to help. Putting together this album will help your person recollect dates, special occasions and other times that hold a special place in his or her memory. You can either put the album together with your person or collect all of the treasures and surprise your person. Either way, this beautiful collection will be treasured.

First Steps

- Gather all the necessary materials: scrapbook, page protectors and pens. Use archival-safe materials. Decide what size is appropriate for your project. Assemble the items that you want to place in the memory album.

- Adhere photos to acid-free cardstock or scrapbooking paper with photo-safe tape runner or adhesive. Place each page in a scrapbook-safe page protector.

✳ Write memories of the event or time period in your best handwriting on pieces of cardstock or directly onto journaling pages. Date the events and experiences that you are writing about.

✳ Attach tickets and small souvenirs directly onto the memory album pages, or set them into vellum or handmade pockets for display and protection.

✳ Decorate the album pages with titles, artwork, stickers and die cuts.

32

CREATE AN ORAL HISTORY

Forgiveness is giving up all hope of having had a different past.
– Unknown

Everyone has a story to tell. When we capture these stories by hand, or on video or recorder, we are holding on to a very special piece of history. An oral history is the systematic process of recording the life experiences of one particular person. Oral histories are based on the human memories of the person being interviewed. There is no right or wrong story when collecting the information. Helping to guide the interview so the stories are told as they happened is the only real challenge. To help in this arena, it is best to plan and organize both questions and items that hold memories for your person. Collect memorabilia such as photos, jewelry, or clothing that spark a remembrance and add to the richness of the history. Each person's narrative creates the patchwork of a family's history for the next generation. More importantly, oral histories highlight our common human experience and bring us closer to one another.

First Steps

❋ Explain to your person what an oral history is and what is expected. If there is profound negativity about the project, don't proceed. Taking an oral history can be a tiring experience for someone who is not onboard with the idea.

✱ Plan the best way to organize the project. Is your subject ready to jump in and just tell stories? Would he like a list of questions to think about? Would she like to collect some photographs to help jog her memory? Also, plan on a date and how long you would like for the interview to last. It is always a good idea to plan 2 sessions – the first one gets the project going; the second one ties everything together.

✱ Decide on the best way to capture the information. Will it be a written history? Or an aural history using a recorder? Or perhaps you could use a video camera. Whichever you choose, keep the process simple.

✱ Move on to the next step once you have your oral history. Use software to create a memoir that includes the oral history with photos and other items inserted into the video. In some instances, "movie making" software can be downloaded free of charge.

✱ Copy everything on to a CD where it can be stored safely once you have your finished product. You might want to consider making extra copies and present them as gifts during the holiday season. An oral history is definitely a gift that keeps on giving.

Note: Check out the oral history questions in the Resource section in the back of the book.

33

TAKE PICTURES

Say Cheese! – Anonymouse

You don't have to call in a professional photographer anymore. Cameras come in all different sizes, shapes and costs. Digital cameras make photography a snap. Throwaway cameras make photography simple and inexpensive. Whatever you choose to bring your subjects to life will work wonders for the morale of your person. Make sure he is looking his best when you take his photo. Make sure she is situated with her loved ones before you take her photo. Let your person be the director of the photos. And don't forget to get Fido the dog or Sam the cat in the shots. Once you have an array of photo memories you can put them in a scrapbook, or go online and have prints made as easily as one, two, three.

First Steps

✳ Create composition – Try taking the picture from a different perspective. Stand on a chair or stool and shoot down on your subject. Get up close and shoot a side view instead of straight on. Or from the back. you'll be seeing your subject from an angle that is bound to create interest.

✳ Move Out of the Comfort Zone – Ask your subject to do something! Show movement, show your person doing something of interest – even smelling a beautiful flower.

✳ Dress up – Pajamas and robes can be attractive, but why not wear a funky hat and a colorful scarf? Try to use props that add color, sparkle and lightness to the photo.

✳ Bring in the canines and the felines – If cats or dogs or birds or lizards live in the same house with your person, bring them out and let them take part in the photo shoot. Nothing adds pizzazz as beautifully as an impromptu lick from a kitten or a puppy. Be prepared to snap it quickly!

✳ Photograph on the sly – Catch your subject when he or she isn't expecting it. Photograph your person when he's reading, or talking with a loved one or sipping hot chocolate. You can end up getting some special shots with your person reacting naturally to any given situation.

✳ And most important – everybody smile!

34

INVOLVE FAMILY MEMBERS IN ACTIVITIES

If the family were a boat, it would be a canoe that makes no progress unless everyone paddles. – Letty Cottin Pogrebin

Sometimes it appears that no one is interested in helping with the caregiving tasks. Often, this assumption is very far from the truth. Many times family members want to help, they just don't know what to do, how to do it – or even how to ask if help is needed. As the primary caregiver, the best way to avoid this confusion is to reach out to others and let them know their help is welcome and very much appreciated. Below are some ideas on how to present options to others.

First Steps

* Start small. Ask family members to come onsite Saturday morning for two hours to manicure the garden, or clean the garage or even complete a simple paint job.

* Create a meal plan for one week. Fill in the names of each family member and evenly distribute the cooking chores. Make sure your plan is equitable. If one person brings the main dish, have another bring some bread and a salad.

* Engage family members who are able to provide massage therapy, hair cutting, manicures, financial or legal

assistance, and call on them for help. Efficient use of resources makes the caregiving tasks easier on everyone.

* Plan a movie night and invite everyone to bring an appetizer or dessert. Select a movie that is light and heartwarming. Allow your person to be the center of attention. Laugh, cry and enjoy the time together.

* Set up a time to Skype with family and friends who do not live close enough to visit often. Be sure to include the teenagers and children. Young people can brighten an elderly or ill person's life with their delightful chatter and amusing stories.

35

UPDATE FAMILY AND FRIENDS REGULARLY

Communication works for those who work at it. – John Powell

Good communication takes work. As a busy caregiver, being asked to take on one more task may feel like you are being over-burdened. But in reality, you won't be. Taking on the role as go-between could be the greatest gift you've been given. Your person's situation governs how much company to receive, how many phone calls to accept, and how much or how little should be shared. Communicating with those who care puts you in the proverbial driver's seat. In essence, you become the editor of your person's life story. Family and friends will appreciate your efforts to keep them informed. Regular communication also serves as a way for you to ask for help, if necessary. Many people want to help; they often just don't know what to do. By including everyone in your person's care, you are building a partnership and a compassionate team.

First Steps

✳ Discuss means of communication with your person. Does he enjoy talking on the phone? Does she prefer writing personal notes? Does he like to receive and answer emails? Is she up on texting? Facebook? Let the likes and dislikes of your person guide the process.

✳ Decide together on frequency of communications. Does she tire easily? Maybe calling her sister once a week is sufficient. Does he have one special friend he likes to share with often? Invite that friend to stop by or call at least twice a week.

✳ Act as mediator if your person isn't able to use email, cell phone or Skype. If your person is comfortable having you in on the conversation, just go with the flow.

✳ Create a one-page newsletter and mail or email it out monthly. Let loved ones know about new medical developments, treatments, outings, visitors, and most of all, positive good health benefits that stem from excellent caregiving. Don't dwell on the negative. Share the activities, procedures, medications that are producing a higher level of quality in your person's life.

✳ Join the Care Page online community at www.carepages.com. There may be a fee associated with this service, but it is worth every dime to anyone facing a life-altering health event. You can relate stories, post photos and relay health updates to family, friends and loved ones. In return, they can send messages of hope, healing and love.

36

ASSIST IN PUTTING AFFAIRS IN ORDER

Put your affairs in order. Your time is nigh! – Unknown

Since none of us really knows exactly when our time is nigh, it is best to be prepared. As caregivers, we can offer an extraordinary service by helping those we serve with putting their affairs in order. This not only provides peace of mind for your person, it also helps family members begin to adjust to the imminent loss of their loved one. Thanks to the Internet, just about everything needed to prepare wills, complete an advance directive or direct organ donations can be downloaded, and mostly free of charge.

First Steps

* Check in with your person's family members and loved ones before launching this project. If these issues are already being tackled, your help might not be needed. If nothing has been done, make an offer to help. Be sure to get permission in writing to proceed.

* Ease into this project by bringing up the subject of putting affairs in order with your person. If he or she doesn't feel comfortable talking about this difficult subject, back off. But remind your person that you will, indeed, bring up the subject again in the near future. Preparing these documents isn't a choice; it's a necessity.

* Make a list of the documents you will need. First on the list should be a will. If a will has already been created, go over every detail to be sure it is up to date.

* Assist in preparation of other important documents including an advance directive, organ donation forms, and revival codes. Some people like to make plans for their own funeral, or discuss whether they would prefer cremation or burial. Be sure to tell designated family member or loved one where all of these documents are kept.

* Initiate discussions about spiritual matters. Would your person like to speak with a priest, minister, rabbi or chaplain? Are there special prayers, hymns or readings your person would like recited either in the hospital or at the funeral? As difficult as this is, planning ahead lightens the grieving process for loved ones.

Note: There is a list of end of life documents in the Resource section at the end of this book.

COMPASSION FATIGUE
AWARENESS PROJECT

SECTION THREE
FOR YOUR ORGANIZATION

Nowhere is it more important to raise levels of compassion satisfaction than in the workplace. When the majority of staff experiences high levels of compassion fatigue, the organization itself becomes compassion fatigued. Symptoms include high levels of Worker's Comp claims, absenteeism, inability for teams to work well together, rampant rumors, and miscommunication between workers and management. Section Three makes useful suggestions on how to raise employee satisfaction scores.

37

DEVELOP EDUCATION FOR STAFF AND VOLUNTEERS

Management means helping people to get the best out of themselves, not organizing things. – Lauren Appley

Employers often fail to recognize that their employees – the people - are their greatest resource. Place workers in a caring, supportive environment and they will give you their best. Place workers in a contentious, competitive environment and they will recoil not only from their workloads, but each other as well. In relation to the helping professions, this lack of a healthy environment affects the bottom line in ways that can't even be measured. The first, and possibly the best, way to encourage and grow your employees is to provide on-the-job education on a regular basis.

First Steps

- Create a company-wide orientation if you don't already have one. Include the history of the organization, the mission statement, introduction to leadership, goals and objectives and any other regulations or rules that apply to your profession. This orientation is mandatory for all new hires.

- Organize monthly Brown Bag luncheon speakers. Be sure to include topics that are of great interest to your staff such as work/play balance, time management and compassion fatigue. Keep the speaker to 45 minutes and allow 10 minutes for Q & A. Put out a call to staff and locate your speakers within the ranks of the organization. This saves times and money.

✻ Assign a well-connected staff member to create company bulletin boards that include the most up-to-date information on your organization, recent media, classes, and memos from management. If done correctly, these bulletins boards become the "go-to" place for staff education.

✻ Ask your CEO to write a company blog 2-3 times weekly. If he or she isn't comfortable writing, go to your Communications Department and assign someone to ghost write the blog. Transparent, open communication from the top is the best way to educate staff in understanding the "bigger picture."

✻ Hold an annual daylong conference for staff. Choose a theme and follow it through with giveaways, speakers and food. It is possible to learn and have fun at the same time. If cost is an issue, hold the conference onsite and half day. Be sure to take photos and post them on your bulletin boards.

38

CREATE AN OUTLET FOR PUBLICLY SHARING BEST PRACTICES

We cannot control the winds, but we can adjust the sails. – Unknown

A best practice is a method or technique that has consistently shown results superior to those achieved with other means, and that is used as a benchmark. According to an article in the Harvard Business Review, it takes an average of two years before a Best Practice winds its way down through an organization. This represents wasted time and energy, not to mention the ability to increase cost savings. Fortunately, in caregiving the process can be made much simpler, especially for home caregivers. Below are 5 Steps in which to promote your positive outcomes to share with family members, friends, and colleagues.

First Steps

✳ Decide on which of the 50 Steps in this book you are going to tackle with your person. Create a template or spreadsheet using a simple metric system such as 1-5, with 1 being the least effective and 5 being the most effective. Leave a space for comments.

✳ Bring out your template or spreadsheet when the project ends and review with your person. Listen as your person assigns a number between 1-5 to every point you present.

* Add up the numbers to determine whether or not the outcome measures up as a benchmark. If numbers are low, ask your person what would have made the Step more beneficial.

* Share your successes with other caregivers through assorted avenues such as Facebook, email, Skype, iPhone, telephone, or in person. Take photos during the process and post them with your explanation of your Best Practice.

* Create a story around your Best Practice and place it in your local newspaper, caregiving publications and newsletters. Sharing with others is one way to escalate the Good News about new caregiving tactics.

39

PROMOTE EMPLOYEE INCENTIVE PROGRAMS

The spirit, the will to win, and the will to excel are the things that endure. These qualities are so much more important than the events that occur.
– Vince Lombardi

Every organization, business or company wants its employees to be motivated and more important, stay motivated. What makes an organization, business or company great is employees who are motivated because they feel valued. Employee incentive programs are one easy way to motivate your workforce. Reward exceptional employees for a job well done, and they will continue their high levels of productivity, creativity and well being. A happy workforce increases the bottom line time and time again. Below are some reasons why incentive programs work and also some ideas for creating one for your caregiving community.

First Steps

* Increase your staff motivation by offering rewards for reaching targets and company goals. When a company cares enough to offer an employee incentive program, everyone wins. Rewards can range from trips to gifts to cash. Make your rewards match up with your company's mission.

* Reduce your absenteeism, turnover rate and high Worker's Compensation claims by offsetting low morale with incentives. When company morale is low, it is possible to take the focus off of management and put it back on staff by involving them in healthy competition.

* Build better teams by offering team incentive programs. Individuals enjoy being singled out for acknowledgement, but so do teams. Offer the winning team a dinner out or free tickets to see a popular movie. If your funding allows, offer each member of the winning team a day off of his or her choice. Nothing motivates employees more than a 3-day weekend.

* Brainstorm to unearth other great ideas for winning employee or teams such as: VIP parking space(s) for a month; tickets for local sporting events; a relaxing, reenergizing day at a spa; a weekend trip to Las Vegas, budget permitting; weekend at a beach house or mountain cabin; gift certificates to a popular restaurant or coffeehouse. If all else fails, cold hard cash is a welcome addition to anyone's paycheck.

* Check that the rules of the game are simple, easy to understand, and pertain to all employees no matter what level in your organization. Fairness tops everything else when it comes to building a happy, loyal workforce.

40
PLANT A COMMON GARDEN AREA

Gardens, scholars say, are the first sign of commitment to a community. When people plant corn they are saying, let's stay here. And by their connection to the land, they are connected to one another. – Anne Raver

A community garden is a single piece of property that is gardened collectively by a group of people. A community garden can be anything the group wants it to be. Fresh fruits and vegetables can be harvested or beautiful cutting flowers as well. Along with the harvest comes a sense of community, a sense of accomplishment, connection to the environment, and a connection with others. I know of a hospital that has a community garden onsite. Their fruits and vegetables are used in the hospital cafeteria and the abundance is shared with a food bank close by. Community gardens even decrease a community's reliance on fossil fuels since the food is grown and disseminated locally. A community garden within your organization promotes good health among your employees by encouraging exercise, a social environment and a break from the daily grind of work. And employees are also treated to an education that can expand far beyond the walls of an office.

First Steps

✳ Put out a call for interested colleagues and, together, create a plan for your garden. Visit other community gardens in your area.

* Approach management as a group and share your ideas and thoughts on how to create a sustainable community garden.

* Locate a plot of land and gain access to use it as your garden.

* Partner with your community to share the costs. Go to your local nursery for plants, vegetables and fruit trees. Hold a fundraiser to purchase garden equipment. Ask your local vintner for used wine barrels for planters. Call your local community colleges and universities to locate Master Gardeners in your area. These folks are knowledgeable, well connected with the agricultural community in your area, and willing to work hard to create a sustainable garden.

* Make a firm commitment to nurture and embellish your community garden. All decisions concerning design, plantings, scheduling work days, maintenance and harvesting your haul are made as a group. Community gardens are ruled by communities.

41

CREATE A BROCHURE ON CAREGIVING

Knowledge is of no value unless you put it into practice.
— Anton Chekhov

Brochures are one way of sharing knowledge in a simple, reader-friendly format that can move others to action. The brochure should contain useful knowledge such as the warning signs of a stroke or heart attack — or it can tell your organization's story in words and pictures. It can be designed and developed in-house to keep costs down, or designed and printed by an ad agency and professional printer. Either way, a brochure is a quick and easy way to spread your good work.

First Steps

✳ Form a committee to decide on the look and content of your brochure. Create the design with your company's branding in mind. Don't forget to include your logo.

✳ Decide on your main message and assign the writing task to someone who can relay ideas simply and creatively.

✳ Tell your story mainly through photographs. Stretch your budget to include a professional photographer to come onsite and shoot casual, but effective, photos of caregiver's providing quality, compassionate care.

✱ Include your spiritual care providers in your brochure if you have chaplains, priests, sisters or brothers on staff. Holistic healing means we treat the whole person – body, mind and spirit.

✱ Distribute your completed brochures throughout your organization and post an electronic version on your Facebook and web site.

42

ARRANGE SPECIAL EMPLOYEE RECOGNITION DAYS

In the arena of human life the honors and rewards fall to those who show their good qualities in action. – Aristotle

The first step in creating an Employee Recognition program is for management to establish criteria for what performance or contribution constitutes rewardable behavior or actions. It is important the management team work together and set up guidelines that are simple and easy to understand. The same "reward" should be given to each recipient. Consistency counts. Under no circumstances should the planning or implementing of this program be designated to executive assistants.

First Steps

* Announce that all employees are eligible for the recognition. Plan some hoopla around the announcement.

* Implement the recognition by supplying the employees with specific information about what behaviors or actions are being rewarded and recognized. Anyone who then performs at the level or standard stated in the criteria receives the reward.

✳ Recognize good work as close to the performance of the actions as possible. This way the recognition reinforces the behavior and serves as a model for others.

✳ Avoid designing a process in which managers "select" the people to receive recognition. This type of process will be viewed forever as "favoritism" or talked about as "it's your turn to get recognized this month." Processes that single out an individual, such as "Employee of the Month," are rarely well-received by staff.

✳ Designate a certain time each month for the recognition event. Again, consistency counts. Employees will make time in their busy workday to attend if they see how important this award is to leadership and management.

43

CELEBRATE SPECIAL OCCASIONS REGULARLY

Nothing makes one more tolerant of a neighbor's noisy party than being there. – Franklin P. Jones

Celebrating as a group serves many purposes. Bringing associates together on a regular basis builds teams, friendships and camaraderie. If celebrations are held on a regular basis the events become part of the corporate culture and are then seen as traditions. The decision as to which occasions to celebrate can be selected via a committee or a company-wide survey. When it comes to caregiving organizations, it is best to hold events every month, or at least once a quarter. The nature of caregiving work can be stressful and tiring. Celebrating your caregiving staff is the best way to let them know you value their commitment and dedication to serving others. Build the cost of the events right into your annual budget. Here are 5 ideas to get you started.

First Steps

    ✳ Recognize your caregivers by holding a monthly birthday party for everyone who has a birthday that month. Instead of the usual birthday cake, hold a birthday breakfast, a late afternoon ice cream sundae making party, or a picnic, weather permitting.

* Form a walking group that meets three times a week, and then share a healthy lunch together. A salad bars or fresh fruit buffet would fill the bill. Be sure to invite those who don't chose to join the walking group to the luncheon.

* Hold an ongoing contest and bring everyone together to announce the winner. Serve light refreshments and keep the winner a secret until the end of the event. One idea: if you have a community bulletin board, have everyone bring his or her baby photo. Number the photos and have staff members fill out a form with their guesses. The person who matches up the most photos with the staff members wins. Prize can be a box of chocolates, a gift card or a beautiful plant for his or her office.

* Plan theme parties around national holidays such as New Year's, Valentine's Day, St. Patrick's Day, 4th of July, Thanksgiving, Hanukkah or Christmas. Decorate appropriately with balloons, seasonal colors, and banners. And don't forget the music to add to the celebratory atmosphere.

* Create invitations and be sure everyone on every shift receives a personal invite. It may be a logistical challenge, but do not forget to include activities and food for the swing shift. Always include a brief heartfelt welcome and thank you from someone in management.

44

INCORPORATE RELIGIOUS HOLIDAYS INTO THE ACTIVITY SCHEDULE

To many people holidays are not voyages of discovery, but a ritual of reassurance. – Philip Andrews

Our religious and spiritual beliefs often define who we are. Every organization consists of staff members from diverse religious or spiritual traditions. And every one of those traditions offers either a day or a season within the calendar year where members follow special observances such as prayers, meditation practices, or food or dress selections. Incorporating these celebrations into your workday not only allows for new friendships and teams to form, but also can provide your workforce with myriad teaching moments.

First Steps

* Take a survey of staff members who want to take part in your religious/spiritual observances. Pass around a worksheet and ask each one to write the name of the holiday, annual dates, special colors, dress, food and music associated with the holiday.

* Bring all of the information to your planning committee and put the dates on a shared calendar. Assign someone the task of researching the holiday or holiday season. As

each holiday arrives, offer an activity such as a breakfast, lunch, snacks, games, or entertainment.

✻ Announce each impending holiday with a flyer, online invite, employee newsletter, posters, and word of mouth. Be sure to invite swing shift employees to attend.

✻ Post photos of each event and display on company bulletin boards. After a certain amount of time, remove the photos and place in a company photo album. This collection will serve as a well-documented history for future workers.

✻ Add a generous line item number to your budget for the following fiscal year so this tradition will continue.

45

GRIEVE TOGETHER

Sometimes someone says something really small and it fits right into this empty place in your heart. – Unknown

Caregivers often work in environments where illness, disease and even death are a daily occurrence. When human loss occurs, the body, mind and soul suffer. Jumpstarting a healthy grief process into action helps heal and repair the brokenness. Spending time alone serves the purpose well. In solitude we are able to go deep inside and bring forth our pain and suffering in order to face it head on and embrace our loss. But grieving with others also serves a purpose by helping us to refocus, reenergize and allow ourselves to lean on the shoulder of another. This is especially true when the trauma of loss is a shared experience in the workplace with colleagues.

First Steps

❋ Form a committee of colleagues who are willing to brainstorm and plan for a process in which colleagues can grieve together. Collect and distribute grief support materials and resources throughout the workplace.

❋ Provide a comprehensive educational workshop on workplace trauma debriefing, stress, burnout, compassion fatigue and the stages of grief. If you feel you aren't qualified to offer this information, find someone in your community who is. The right person might be found in the Chaplain Services department at your local hospital or at a nearby hospice.

❋ Create a welcoming healing environment that is only used for grief support (see # 47). Be inclusive in selecting décor and surroundings. Be respectful and aware of diverse faith traditions and individual spiritual journeys.

❋ Offer a colleague in need support by offering to share his or her workload or help on a special project, make a nutritious lunch for two and share, carpool so your colleague doesn't have the stress of driving.

❋ Most of all, be sensitive to the needs of others during difficult times. Provide a listening ear, when appropriate. Remember to practice authentic, sustainable self-care when experiencing a traumatic stress incident. Helping others is effective only when we care for ourselves as well. If your organization provides an emergency and/ or trauma center in your community, educate staff to share their feelings as opposed to telling the stories of the traumatic events they have witnessed. Sharing feelings won't re-traumatize colleagues. Unfortunately, sharing the details could create more trauma in the workplace.

46

START A SUPPORT GROUP

No one can whistle a symphony. It takes a whole orchestra to play it.
– H.E. Luccock

Organizing a support group might be the best thing you can do for your staff members. Bringing caregivers together weekly on a regular basis can provide the understanding, hope and healing that makes a difference in their lives. If it is possible to afford a professional facilitator, such as a psychologist or a therapist, definitely bring that person onboard. Most support groups are run by volunteers without any fees charged to participants. It is helpful if the person who oversees the group has some coaching or counseling experience. More than anything, it is imperative that person be able to control the group and be sure everyone has a voice that is heard and validated. To begin the process of creating a viable support group, there are a number of things that will be helpful.

First Steps

- Distribute a regular newsletter and place a brief article informing staff about the formation of a support group. List the specifics such as where, when and who to contact.

- Bring a special guest speaker onboard for the initial meeting could bring more interested parties to the group. Invite someone who understands the dynamics of caregiving and also can impart some wisdom as far as creating a successful, sustainable support group.

✻ Invite caregivers from local helping professions, place a flyer with pertinent information at the library, and on church, school and community bulletin boards. If you have access to a community television station, inquire about creating a Public Service Announcement (PSA).

✻ Place the information about the group in the datebook section of your local newspaper. Contact the editor or a health reporter and inform him or her about your group. Suggest the reporter write an article and interview the organizers.

✻ Ask creative members of the group to design a brochure that can be distributed throughout the community. Ask your organization to donate the funding to print the brochures.

✻ Note: For more information about organizing and managing a support group, go to the American Self-Help Group Clearinghouse at www.selfhelpgroups.org.

47

CREATE A QUIET PLACE TO DEBRIEF

Courage doesn't always roar. Sometimes courage is the quiet voice at the end of the day saying, "I will try again tomorrow." – Mary Anne Radmacher

Post crisis debriefing led by an educated, knowledgeable facilitator enables caregivers to return to their daily routine with less chance of experiencing post traumatic stress disorder (PTSD). The intervenor, as this person is often called, can bring a person or a group of persons who have witnessed a traumatic incident back to a calm reality, if the debriefing occurs within 72 hours of the event. Traumatic events can bring up powerful emotions, but with a trained intervenor, self-care and time, the exposed caregivers can return to their normal lives without the damage trauma can incur.

First Steps

❊ Claim an area in your building where team members can create a calm and quiet environment where staff can debrief, if necessary. Make sure the area can be shut off from the rest of the staff members. Ensure solitude and sound proofing.

❊ Stock the room with items that soothe and heal. Tea, natural fruit juices, hot chocolate and simple cookies and crackers make light snacks to calm nerves. Also have Kleenex on hand.

✲ Invest in a trained intervenor who can arrive onsite quickly. Or provide training for an employee who is interested in taking on the role.

✲ When the group gathers to debrief, brainstorm methods of coping mechanisms. Share feelings, but not traumatic details of the incident. Listen carefully as each participant speaks and offer gentle words of support.

✲ Implement a follow-up procedure days and weeks following the debriefing. Refer any participant who is beginning to experience the symptoms of PTSD to a mental health professional.

Note: To learn more about critical incident debriefing, go to the International Critical Incident Stress Foundation at www. icisf.org.

48

DEVELOP A CORPORATE WELLNESS PROGRAM

The groundwork of all happiness is good health. – Unknown

The only way organizational compassion fatigue can be minimized or avoided is through management buy in. Staff can do everything in their power to create a healthy workplace, but if they don't have the support of management, the program won't be sustainable. If you take your organization's mission statement and place it up against the symptoms of compassion fatigue, both individual and organizational, you will find that high levels of compassion fatigue in the workplace will undermine your mission statement in myriad ways. When this happens, it won't be long before the bottom line is affected. And for any organization to be successful both its mission and staff values must align. One of the most viable ways to succeed is by creating a Corporate Wellness Program.

First Steps

❋ Solicit input. Open up the discussion by keeping staff informed of the plans to start a Corporate Wellness Program. Don't tell them what you are going to do, ask them what they would like to see in the workplace. Gather all of their suggestions and choose those which are practical and sustainable.

* Start in the cafeteria. What better way to show your employees you care than by offering nutritious food at a reasonable price? This is easily accomplished by setting up a healthy salad bar chock full of fresh vegetables and fruits. You might even offer a vegetarian menu one day a week.

* Encourage healthy change. Welcome self-help organizations such as Ash Kickers for smoking and Weight Watchers for weight loss to your workplace. Allow staff members to take time off of work to attend their weekly or monthly meetings. Self improvement practices make stronger, more focused workers.

* Create support groups onsite. Invite presenters from organizations such as Diabetes Support, Deep Breathers and Mindfulness Stress Reduction programs to present one hour workshops. Hold the workshops at lunchtime and urge your employees to bring a healthy Brown Bag lunch.

* Provide staff with Wellness services such as an Employee Assistance Program, free blood pressure checks, annual flu vaccines, and if possible, discounted gym memberships.

49

HOLD EMPLOYEE FORUMS

Education is all a matter of building bridges. – Ralph Ellison

The main objective of holding employee forums is to build bridges. If done right, management speaking openly, clearly and with transparency can create a cohesive workplace environment. No matter the size of the organization, getting together on a regular basis to get everyone on the same page is a positive management move. And don't hold back on the information. Chris Piling, Head of Direct Banking at HBSC suggests "if you want your people to work with you and really buy in to what you are trying to achieve, you need to treat them like adults – give them the information and trust them to help you develop and implement solutions." Regular forums can achieve this goal.

First Steps

* Encourage leadership to take a workshop or course in public speaking. Your employee Forum won't be of interest to your employees if the presenter doesn't have speaking and presenting skills and stumbles through the material.

* Include employees from all shifts – day and night. If it isn't possible to have management stay on into the evening hours to present to the night shift, have the Forum videotaped by a professional. Organize a time

and place where the Forum will be shown to those who missed the live presentation.

❊ Provide refreshments. Nothing brings a staff together faster and more happily than food. Put lots of nutritious snacks on the menu! This reminds your employees that you not only care about their productivity and skills, you care about their health and well being.

❊ Create a welcoming environment. If forums are held every quarter, decorate with a seasonal theme. The fall season is a good time to start. There is nothing more festive than pumpkins, fall leaves and hot cider to bring people together. Seasonal décor is a small investment that reaps high scores with employees.

❊ Design an assessment tool to provide you with feedback. Management may think it has done a terrific job, but it's the employees who need to be pleased. A survey is always the simplest and most forthright method of assessment. Create a survey on SurveyMonkey.com. It's free and it's easy.

50

CELEBRATE LIFE

God made man because he loves stories. – Elie Wiesel

Human beings are born storytellers. What better way to celebrate our lives than by sharing our stories? Remember, caregiving consists of giving and receiving. Listen well as your person or colleagues share his or her stories, but in turn, request his or her attention as you tell your stories. For every action there is a reaction. In your reaction to each other, a partnership forms and grows. And soon it becomes apparent that no matter our age, gender, nationality or life experiences, there comes a moment when our paths cross and a deep understanding takes hold. We may laugh, cry, agree or disagree. But in this unique form of sharing, our humanity surfaces and we realize that underneath it all, we are all the same. And in this new awareness, we are called to celebrate.

First Steps

* Always choose to be present.

* Always choose to be aware.

* Always choose to be mindful.

* Always choose to be receptive.

* And most important, always choose to celebrate life.

A FINAL WORD

I hope *Compassion Satisfaction: 50 Steps to Healthy Caregiving* has sparked an interest in creating new and helpful ways in which to provide care to others. If you have attempted to put into action any of the ideas in this book, you probably have a better sense of what a true partnership entails: caregiving is about giving and receiving. Hopefully, you have experienced both sides of this unique fellowship. And more important, I hope the ideas expressed in this book will spur you on to design and implement your own gentle ways to aid in the healing process of those in pain and who are suffering. It is my hope that you will share this book with your family members, friends and colleagues. Perhaps they, too, will be energized in knowing there is more than one road to quality, compassionate caregiving. Each one of us is called to serve and forge his or her own exceptional path. And in doing so, we promote and bring out the best in others and in ourselves. Together, acting on our empathy and compassion for others, we learn and we observe. We create a memory album for a child with a life-threatening illness. We bring music to the room of a critically ill teenager. We gather a spa basket for a woman who has lost all of her hair due to chemotherapy. We write diligently as an elderly dying man tells his life story.

And in these very human interactions, we are filled.

RESOURCES

NOTES

#22 ENCOURAGE GOOD GROOMING PRACTICES

Spa/Gift Basket Items

* Pedicure Basket: Foot brush, foot roller, soothing foot cream, foot soak, exfoliating foot scrub, leg rub, re-energizing foot spray, spa slippers, nail file, and polish.

* Bath Basket: Soothing bubble bath, lightly-scented body lotion, bath pillow, exfoliating body net, non-allergenic oatmeal or honey soap, and eye mask.

* Ladies Basket: Lightly scented body powder, body butter, French-milled cleansing soap, gel eye mask, loofah body net, bath pillow, soft terrycloth towel and bath robe.

* For Her Hands Only Basket: Healing soap, lightly-scented hand soak, buffer, nail file, polish remover, polish, cuticle oil, manicure gloves.

* Gentleman's Basket: Small grooming kit, body wrap, back massager, spa slippers, shaving cream and lotion.

* Healthy Snack Basket: Trail mix, apple chips and other dried fruits, raisins, organic crackers, roasted nuts, granola bars, 100% fruit juice.

#32 CREATE AN ORAL HISTORY

50 Oral History Questions:

1) What is your full name? Why did your parents select this name for you? Did you have a nickname?

2) When and where were you born?

3) How did your family come to live there?

4) Were there other family members in the area? Who?

5) What was the house (apartment, farm, etc.) like? How many rooms? Bathrooms? Did it have electricity? Indoor plumbing? Telephones?

6) Were there any special items in the house that you remember?

7) What is your earliest childhood memory?

8) Describe the personalities of your family members.

9) What kind of games did you play growing up?

10) What was your favorite toy and why?

11) What was your favorite thing to do for fun?

12) Did you have family chores? What were they? Which was your least favorite?

13) Did you receive an allowance? How much? Did you save your money or spend it?

14) What was school like for you as a child? What were your best and worst subjects? Where did you attend grade school? High school? College?

15) What school activities and sports did you participate in?

16) Do you remember any fads from your youth? Popular hairstyles? Clothes?

17) Who were your childhood heroes?

18) What were your favorite songs and music?

19) Did you have any pets? If so, what were their names?

20) What was your religion growing up? What church, if any, did you attend?

21) Were you ever mentioned in a newspaper?

22) Who were your friends when you were growing up?

23) What world events had the most impact on you while you were growing up? Did any of them personally affect your family?

24) Describe a typical family dinner. Did you all eat together as a family? Who did the cooking? What were your favorite foods?

25) How were holidays (birthdays, Christmas, etc.) celebrated in your family? Did your family have special traditions?

26) How is the world today different from what it was like when you were a child?

27) Who was the oldest relative you remember as a child? What do you remember about them?

28) What do you know about your family surname?

29) Is there a naming tradition in your family, such as always giving the firstborn son the name of his grandfather?

30) What stories have come down to you about your parents? Grandparents? More distant ancestors?

31) Are there any stories about famous relatives in your family?

32) Have any recipes been passed down to you from family?

33) Are there any physical characteristics that run in your family?

34) Are there any special heirlooms, photos, bibles or other memorabilia that have been passed down in your family?

35) What was the full name of your spouse? Siblings? Parents?

36) When and how did you meet your spouse? What did you do on dates?

37) What was it like when you proposed (or were proposed to)? Where and when did it happen? How did you feel?

38) Where and when did you get married?

39) What memory stands out the most from your wedding day?

40) How would you describe your spouse? What do (did) you admire most about them?

41) What do you believe is the key to a successful marriage?

42) How did you find out your were going to be a parent for the first time?

43) Why did you choose your children's names?

44) What was your proudest moment as a parent?

45) What did your family enjoy doing together?

46) What was your profession and how did you choose it?

47) If you could have had any other profession what would it have been? Why wasn't it your first choice?

48) Of all the things you learned from your parents, which do you feel was the most valuable?

49) What accomplishments were you the most proud of?

50) What is the one thing you most want people to remember about you?

Note: Questions reprinted from www.about.com/geneology

#36 ASSIST IN PUTTING AFFAIRS IN ORDER

Important Documents:

- Car Title
- House Title
- Mortgage Papers
- Property Tax Statements
- Medicare Card
- Supplemental Health Policies
- Long-Term Care Policy
- Life Insurance Policy
- Bank or Investment Statements
- Certificates Of Deposit
- Social Security Papers
- Pensions or Veteran's Retirement Benefits
- Medical Statements
- List Of Valuables
- Living Trust
- Will/Codicil (Addendum To Will)
- Advanced Directive
- Living Will
- Funeral/Memorial Plan & Expenses
- Birth Certificate & Death Certificate Information
- Prewritten Obituary

Note: Information from *Dare To Care: Caring For Our Elders* by Cheryl Carmichael

SUGGESTED READING LIST

Carmichael, Cheryl; *Dare to Care: Caring for our Elders*

Chapman, Erie; *Radical Loving Care*

Collinge, William, MD; *Partners in Healing: Simple Ways to Offer Support, Comfort and Care to a Loved One Facing Illness*

Gantner, Dr. Rose Karlo, Ed.D: *Workplace Wellness: Performance with a Purpose: Achieving Health Dividends for Employers and Employees*

Hart, Cynthia, Lisa Sampson: *The Oral History Workshop: Collect and Celebrate the Life Stories of Your Family and Friends*

McBee, Lucia, LCSW MPH: *Mindfulness-Based Elder Care: A CAM Model for Frail Elders and Their Caregivers*

Myss, Caroline, C. Norman M.D. Shealy: *The Creation of Health: The Emotional, Psychological, and Spiritual Responses That Promote Health and Healing*

Nettle, Claire: *Growing Community: Starting and Nurturing Community Gardens*

Schachter-Shalomi, Zalman, Ronald S. Miller: *From Age-ing to Sage-ing: A Profound New Vision of Growing Older*

Schulte, Mary S.: *Fun Party Themes for Seniors*

Seiser, Lynn: *Trauma, Trance and Treatment*

Torrance, Hal: *Activities for the Senior Mind: Keeping Your Brain Exercised and Sharp*

MY HEALTHY CAREGIVING STEPS

This is a place to record your thoughts, beliefs and successes. Visit these pages often.

ABOUT THE AUTHOR

Patricia Smith is the founder of the Compassion Fatigue Awareness Project and Healthy Caregiving, LLC.

As a certified Compassion Fatigue Specialist with more than 20 years of training experience, she writes, speaks and facilitates workshops in service of those who care for others in all caregiving professions. With a background in journalism, Patricia's writing has appeared in numerous publications, including the San Jose Mercury News where she was a freelance journalist for more than 20 years. She is the Caregiving Expert for Spry Living magazine, reaching millions of readers every month. As training and development manager for the Humane Society Silicon Valley, she created and implemented a critical shelter-wide compassion fatigue project. Her work in this field led to presenting workshops nationwide as a consultant for American Humane, a national organization advocating children and animal rights.

She is the recipient of the "Excellence in Writing Award" presented by the National League of American Pen Women; and, under her direction, the Ronald McDonald House at Stanford received the 2005 "Best Bets" award for its "Healing Arts" program, which Patricia developed there.

Through the Compassion Fatigue Awareness Project, Patricia has authored two training manuals, a presenter's guide, and a student workbook. Her book *To Weep for a Stranger: Compassion Fatigue in Caregiving* is a comprehensive look at compassion fatigue, its causes and symptoms, and how to begin the healing process.

She can be reached at patricia@compassionfatigue.org or www.facebook.com/compassionfatigue.

Made in the USA
San Bernardino, CA
25 January 2016